Rabbit's Tail

Duncan Williamson and Linda Williamson

Illustrated by David Parkins

 CAMBRIDGE
UNIVERSITY PRESS

Once upon a time, Rabbit had two little ears and a beautiful big tail. He didn't look like rabbits do today! When he walked through the forest and met his little friends, he would say to them, "Wouldn't you like to have a nice tail like mine?"

Oh, Rabbit was so proud!

Well, one winter morning all the little creatures got together. They said, "We can't go on like this. Something must be done about Rabbit's boasting."

Hedgehog said, "What shall we do? He's bigger than us." Then she said, "I've got an idea. Let's go and see our friend Fox. He's very clever."

So off they went together to the hillside. And they found Fox asleep in his den, with his head on his paws. They shouted, "Wake up, Fox, we've come to see you."

"Fox, you're the wisest creature of all. We need your help. It's Rabbit," said the animals.

Fox said, "Oh dear. There are many things I'd like to do with Rabbit if I could catch him! What kind of help do you want from me?"

Hedgehog said, "Rabbit keeps boasting about his tail all day long. We're just fed up listening to him."

Fox said, "Well, just give me a day or two to think about it."

So off they went, back to the forest. They knew their friend Fox would help them.

Two days later, Fox was walking along the
riverside when he found a big fish. A fisherman had
dropped it from his bag. And, of course, Fox picked
it up in his mouth.

At that moment, who should come poppety, poppety, poppety, down the hillside? Rabbit, with his great big, bushy tail held up in the air. When he saw Fox, he stopped.

He said, "Hey, Foxy! Is that a fish you've got
there?"

Then Fox had an idea. He placed the fish very
carefully between his paws. He said, "Of course it's
a fish, Rabbit! I've caught this for my breakfast."

Rabbit said, "Oh, Foxy, can you spare a little bit for me? I love fish, too, you know!"

"Indeed not!" said Fox. "Do you think that I'm going to spend all night long out here, sitting in the cold, to catch a fish and share it with you? If you want a fish, catch one for yourself!"

And Rabbit said, "How do you catch a fish, Fox?"

Fox said, "No problem, Rabbit. Tonight, when
the moon comes up and it gets very cold, you come
down to the river. Find a nice little pool, put in
your tail and wait till a little fish comes along and
nibbles on it. Pull out your tail and you'll have a
fish just like mine!" And Fox, laughing to himself,
went off to his den.

Rabbit watched him for a little while and said, "Fox thinks he's smart, doesn't he? I'm just as clever as he is! Tonight I'll catch a fish and I'll have it all to myself."

That night, when the moon came up, it was very
cold. Rabbit had a lovely fur coat to keep him
warm. He came down to the riverside, found a
little, deep pool, turned around and put his long,
bushy tail in the water.

There he sat and waited. Soon, he would have
a fish for himself.

The moon rose high in the sky and it got colder
and colder.

At that moment, who should come walking up
the riverside but Jack Frost, with his long, spiky nose
and his spiky fingers! He was turning all the water
into ice, freezing all the pools, making all the icicles.

He walked past the pool where Rabbit sat with
his tail in the water, and he laughed to himself.
But Rabbit knew nothing of this, for no-one sees
Jack Frost.

Rabbit sat all night long until the moon went down and the sun came up. He rubbed his eyes.

"Aha, there must be a fish on my tail by this time!" said Rabbit. He tried to pull his tail from the river, but . . . aargh! Jack Frost had frozen the pool solid!

"Help me, someone, help me!" cried Rabbit as he pulled and tugged.

Then, at that moment, who should come walking up but Stork, with her long legs and her long beak.

When she saw Rabbit, she said, "Hey, Rabbit, why are you crying? What's all the noise about?"

"Oh, Stork, you must help me!" begged Rabbit. "My beautiful tail is caught in the ice and I can't get free."

"Oh dear," said Stork. Now, a stork is a very kindly bird. "I will help you," she said.

And with her big, long beak she caught Rabbit by his tiny little ears and she pulled.

But Rabbit's tail was still trapped in the ice. Stork tugged and tugged. Rabbit's ears began to stretch; they got longer and longer.

Then, SNAP! Rabbit's tail broke and left just a tiny little stump. Rabbit was free, but his beautiful tail had gone.

"Oh! I can't go back to the forest again and see all my little friends," said Rabbit. "They'll laugh at me."

So he ran to the hillside and dug-dug-dug himself a burrow. There he hid.

Back in the forest, the little creatures said,
"I wonder what's happened to Rabbit? He hasn't
come back to boast about his tail."

But Rabbit's beautiful tail had gone for ever.
Instead, he had two big, long ears. He felt so
ashamed of himself that he stayed in his burrow.

And the years passed. Hundreds of years passed
by. And still to this day, all the little rabbits have
two big ears and a little, short tail!